Liberation Songs

Monica Czubba

BookLeaf Publishing

India | USA | UK

Presentation by *BookLeaf Publishing*

Web: www.bookleafpub.com

E-mail: info@bookleafpub.com

ISBN: 9789360943707

First edition 2024

To Justin, for always being there.

ACKNOWLEDGEMENT

Free Palestine

My Favorite Hiding Place

My childhood home had the best hiding place
In an upstairs bedroom, in the closet to the left
Behind clothes you'd find the plywood-covered
entrance
To a private Narnia where secrets were kept
If secrets were benign shoeboxes of bad poetry
and blurry photos

Next to my older brothers' Star Wars Ewok
Village and G.I. Joe fleet
Sat my blanket nest filled with crumpled paper
balls, old snacks, and art
After the space became mine, their memories
remained
A collection of childhoods, separately full of
heart
But their collections were arguably more
valuable than mine

Yet it was when hiding from seekers—this place
taught me about "winning"
To do so without effort, my joy escaped my
purpose, my success was redefined
My solution working didn't make it right, even I
knew that then

Sometimes in our world, for joy, cooperation
must be outlined
Unfortunately, for more than just 8-year-olds
and their hiding places

Remain Dangerously Hopeful

When I was young, like many
I thought I knew more than I did
As I sat, a shitty variable on the Dunning-Kruger
effect
Lapping up millennial encouragement
Convinced in my convictions
I was dangerously hopeful

I waded through trauma, lost my youth
Bearing witness to societal evolution at warp
speed
Somehow still determined to beat the odds
When everything seems against it
We were going to change the world
When did you find out it was a lie?

Standing at the point of no return
Challenging the inevitability of suffering
How do we move past this without more pain
With the innovative imagination of hopeful souls
Going on, and on, and on, and on…
As this work is never done, unlike what were fed

Now is the time to re-script our stories

We've landed on the right side of history,
humanity
Inheriting the world, we must rebuild her
structure
Remain dangerously hopeful in our convictions
Heal the collective, connect the community
I'm dangerously hopeful we can still beat the
odds

The Everlasting Sweater

I keep this old sweater my mother gave me
It's not the only thing I have left that was a gift
For some reason which I cannot pinpoint
It stands out above all the rest

It reminds me of her hugs, enveloping, not
suffocating
In a simple cream, classic and lovely
Why this loosely crocheted sweater means so
much
Even if I only wear it less than five times a year

I get compliments when it makes an appearance
I get condolences when I answer where I got it
This inexplicable duality of presence and lack
thereof
Live on in everything I do without her

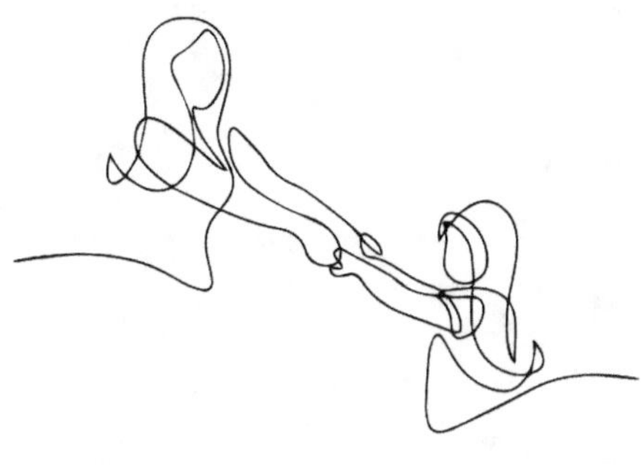

I don't think I can ever rid myself of it
Her motherhood remains in the gifts she gave
me, but
I'll never know if the weighted comfort of it
calms me
Or the weight that she gave it to me that keeps
me calm

A Midnight Greyhound

As I sat in an empty station somewhere in
Detroit
I felt like a ghost on a solo trip
Manually breathing, in a trance and alone
When from behind I'm met with a quip

A stranger, well dressed, with no fear at all
Introduces themselves to the only other patron
At a Greyhound station in the middle of the
night
Striking up friendly conversation

I learned he was a doctor, traveling for work
He learned I lost a loved one, traveling to grieve
The stranger may never know how much those
hours meant
Nurtured human connection, a needed reprieve

He made a note to stay until my connection
arrived
Although I'd argue the connection was made
I wonder if like me, that man remains
Rapt with this memory that just won't fade

Under the Umbrella

As I watch you play in the dirt from afar
I wonder how much longer I can keep you there
In that space of limitless joy
Brought on by a handful of sand

Exclaiming in triumph with every throw
Fully expelling all breath in your chest
Experiencing something with your whole being
Exhilarated at every new sensation

I can't help but let out a deep belly laugh
As you run back to me with your newest treasure
A rock—just for me—tan and smooth all around
I might just keep it forever

A stone picked by you for me is the very best
kind

To remember this moment for the rest of my
days
For the truth is, I can't keep us here and in this
moment
So let us enjoy our stone and our shade

Hues and Hopes

Childlike giggles float in summer air
Each breath giving life to soapy planets for play
Leaving polka-dot prints on the concrete
Rainbow bubbles, wet and shining
Each sailing a uniquely curious way

Knowing no boundaries which limit and silence
Silly pokes and jovial notes follow the spheres
around
Clambering high, free falling low
In the simplest of smiles, a true model of joy
Surviving the turbulence 'til finding the ground

In these tides and currents of hues and hopes
There's no measure for happiness, but if there
must be
I'd imagine a meter as sweet as this scene
Searching through a symbiosis of colors and
light
A kaleidoscopic emotional sea

Connection

When I walk outside and look up high
I close my eyes and I ask
"Honey, send some lovin' my way"
With no beat skipped my world flips
As the clouds drift away
You make the sun shine bright again

Even far away I feel it
Wherever it was that you went
But I know deep down
From the ground to my crown
You're always there
Pushing the clouds away

I think I've finally learned
That it's not heartache, but a current
One that always flows and transmits

Sometimes gentle, sometimes stronger
Isn't that a beautiful thought
That the universe keeps us all together

In a Single Breath

What makes the air fresh?
The external clash with nature
It's effortless recycling untethered
Wild, fierce, uncaptured

What makes nature wild?
Informal governance guiding life
By unknown cultures without borders
Determined, unbothered, free

What makes life meaningful?
Unconditional empathy carrying hearts
Purpose-driven collective action
Hopeful, fearless, ready

Hand in Hand

Sharp blades of grass
Young, strong, and new
My fingers brush over them
A cool breeze rushes through

Wind whips sunburnt cheeks
Awakening me from the haze
With dirt, pollen, or an errant insect
On these sweltering Spring days

Leaning back on the chain link fence
Weaving weeds through the mesh
One flying ant—no, two, maybe three
Crawling on, inspecting, my flesh

Dirt on my knuckles, under my nails
Working the earth, playing with sand
Muscles ache from recycling life
The land and I, hand in hand

Connecting with nature
Honoring the past
Fostering a future
In which we all can last

Losing Myself

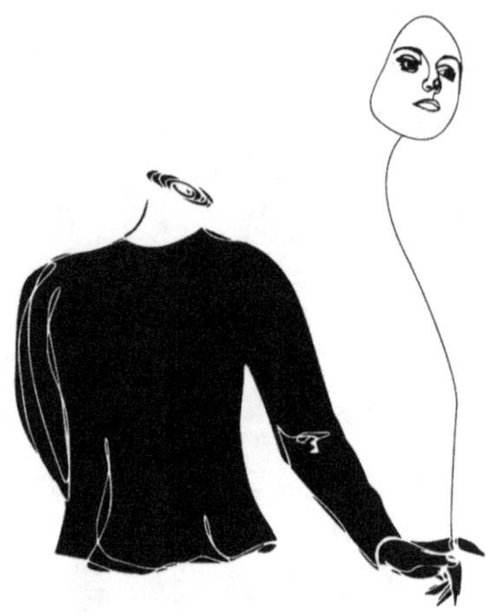

Losing my memories to trauma
Is like watching a large fishing net
Collect without regard to life
Scooping up everything in its path
Whether it's meant to or not

Losing my body to trauma
Is a literal out-of-body experience
Seeing the world entirely in third person
Sensory differentiation becomes impossible
Seeking relief at every turn

Losing my heart to trauma
Is the hardening of my emotions
The calcification of connection

Feeling lost amongst the crowd
With no strength left to fight it

Losing my soul to trauma
Is a rebirth I didn't know I needed
I'd prefer to have never known its grasp
But as it lingered… I learned
So I will never lose myself again

Within All of Us

Within all of us is a mystical force
Present to empower us with affect
A change prepared to disenthrall
Those lost to the mesmerism of self

Within all of us is an ethereal soul
Beating to the eurythmics of community
Demanding to be set free from bondage
Placed upon them by individualism

Within all of us is a human being
Seeking connection within society
Wanting to have a place to thrive
Safe from the clutches of capitalism

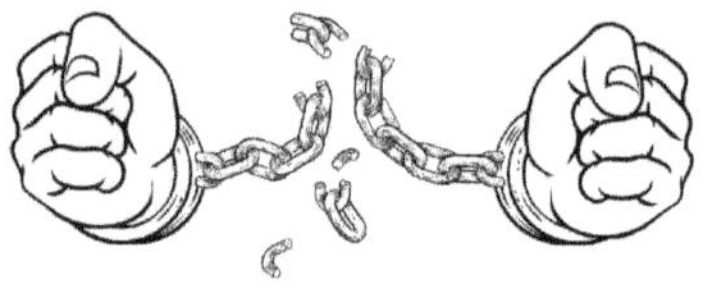

Within all of us is a unique identity
Outside of the norms of patriarchal society
Ready to thrive beyond in a future
Where we've evolved beyond redundancy

Within all of us is a light burning bright
Yearning to burn down white supremacy
Calling for an end to the reign of ignorance
To see us through the darkness

Within all of us is the ability to grow
To be beckoned to open our eyes
To challenge our senses, to shake our hearts
To move our bodies towards the light of
liberation

Personally Political

In bustling streets where politics reigns
Amidst the chaos, society's strain
Lies a tapestry of small human scenes
Moments—fleeting—where souls convene

In corridors of power, voices clash
Ideals collide, ambitions dash
In the middle of this personal fray
Lives intertwine in the everyday

A mother kisses her child goodbye
A worker strives beneath a hot sky
In the rhythm, life's transient beat
Small moments of connection, tender and sweet

Among active protests, when rallies resound
In the cacophony of voices, becoming drowned
A whisper of kindness, a touch of grace
As strangers who meet in an unexpected space

Between ideals clashing, we strangers must unite
In the quest for justice and equity, we must
ignite
In those small moments, waiting, our power lies

Ready to reshape the world beneath her vast
skies

Shatter their barriers with radical empathy
Challenge their norms with unyielding solidarity
For in these acts, rebellious and keen
Lies the essence of the societal scene, unseen

Fury Over Power

A silent fury overflows the shadows
The shadows of a frustrating past
A past to be nothing but ashamed of
For shame marks the place of last

Last has its advantages
Advantages of a new point of view
A view that has one simplistic goal
The goal of inspiring you

Inspiring you is a greater power than most
For most just quietly, cynically, and judge
Judgment answers nothing in this world
A world of chronic pain and suffering

Physical suffering is nothing in retrospect
Retrospect to the pain the heart feels
These feelings drive us to live on
Living on, to love and give

Giving nothing, take nothing in this world
This world needs a new beginning
Beginning again is all we can do now
For now we don't need to fear fake power

Remembering

In a flash
Becoming anchored to the past
Timekeeper nowhere to be found
The relay station provides no response
Relevance in presence dissipates
Depersonalization sets in

Disassociation conquers fears
Strength of self-preservation prevails
Bodily sensations numb without substance
The memories take charge
Reality breaks
But feeling alive

Just as fast
From action to where emotion should be
An empathetic parasympathetic system
Imbalanced yet functioning
Just enough to hide the grief
Mourning and healing

One day it will be different
Feelings will be deeply felt
The body will feel secure
That future is not today
So we carry on remembering

Manifestos

As society honors the obedient
The innocents suffer from genocide
Our microcosm experiment is flailing
While all we have left seems lost
At what cost?
Relying on general observations practices
economic futility
Concise ramblings will grab a foothold
Yet the end seems so far off
Our ability to be warm and subjective proves
trite
Are we still right?
As a whole we are the assailants
As the individual we are tragically chaotic
Not even able to hold a steady hand
The attempt to be hopeful cynically dies
Do we hear the cries?

A beginning is needed
We all need to run
The time for amusement, depleted
Don't turn back as you flee the wasteland
Need a hand?
This quagmire—this cesspool has grown large
enough
There is only one catch to this chance
Grab another to carry on your back
Loyalties may fade as the reset button is hit
How far can we get?

Enduring

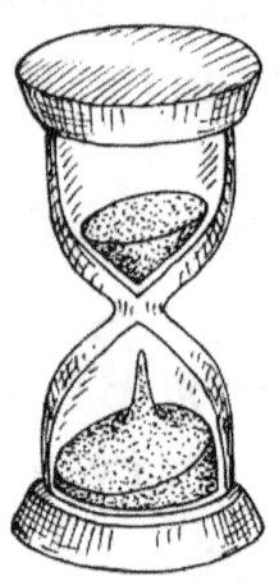

If nothing is taught, then nothing is learned
Though everyone knows what we all yearn
The ambiguity of hope weaves intrigue around
And we'll look to the sky as it sits on the ground

Confused we may become and simple we may
be
But there is no true reason for why we cannot
see
Our blindness consumes us, our feelings deceive
When our minds cannot see through the knots
and the weaves

It's unfortunate to learn that throughout the years
We're not meant to know, but to only shed tears
Life too often defined by loss, pain and suffering
alarm

Everyone to realize how poorly we deal with
harm

Life cannot be lived with what we've been
taught
Because everything we've lost has been
everything we've sought
If nothing is accomplished before our
preemptive expiration
The sure thing to remember is to deny
exasperation

So as to win in any terms we must fight and love
at one time
And carry our weight to the sweet end but to
never look behind
Yet nothing has more precedence than the ability
to aid and love
It's a test to prove why we're here, that nothing
else better waits above

Let Darkness Be Missed

Walls have collapsed
The world breaking down
Barriers have been broken
No one makes a sound

Witnessing the crumbling
What will be done
Now there is no one
No songs will be sung

Dared to step up
Challenge the norm
How to combat it?
What is its form?

Wishes of luck
For walking in blind
Some might say
That's being too kind

Not kind enough
Not a sense through human eyes
Looking to fight
To answer the cries

Move up and forward
And promise just this
Keep kicking 'til daylight
Let darkness be missed

Never Rest Your Case

In defense of humanity
And what our bones remember
A call to free us all
And to leave empires in embers

Prisoners of our geography
Where the people cannot rule
Noise becomes the goal
Empowering the tools and fools

The randomness of their noise
Fleeting from control
Their biases remain predictable
If still a killer of the soul

See through the propaganda
Cut through the noise
Scream with your whole being
Stand proudly with poise

In the silence, find your strength
Amidst the clamor, hear your voice
Resonate with truth and justice
Make empathy your choice

Together, we can dismantle
The structures built on fear
Embrace the power of unity
Let compassion steer

In the echo of our actions
Let empathy resound
In the heart of every struggle
Humanity shall be found

Why We Must

When others call to be heard
Over injustices thrust upon them
Restore humanity word by word
To promise that their story will be told
This is why we must

When others are at the mercy of a lesser evil
Be unwilling to accept evil at all
Bear witness to others and sit with it still
To commit to everlasting empathy
This is why we must

When we become numb to the trauma and the
grief

In a buzzing crowd of blurry imagery
Reconnect with the self, a brief reprieve
To move our bodies towards liberation
This is why we must

When future generations inherit loss or
prosperity
They will have only what was left behind
Provide willingly, unconditionally
To be an honorable ancestor
This is why we must

Liberation Song

In shadows of ancient olive trees
Where Sunbirds dance upon the breeze
A symphony of resistance sung far and wide
Upon lands where red poppies thrive

Admits the rubble, a spirit unbroken
Voice raised, in defiance spoken
Witness the unyielding fight
For freedom's dawn in the darkest night

Anger simmering beneath the surface
The deafening silence, with or without purpose
Politics of indifference, a betrayal profound
As unending cries for humanity resound

In the hearts of those who want more to be
A stirring, a beckoning, to do more than see
For in bearing truth, we find our part
In the liberation of every heart

Hope flickers like a flame in the black of the
night
Guiding forward, towards what's right
Through chaos and through pain
To a world where justice reigns

Stand tall, stand firm, stand in solidarity
With the spirit and strength of resilient ferocity
When faced with the oppressor we shall rise
strong
In the heart of our Liberation Song